PARANORMAL LIFE CYCLES

ZOMBIE

By
Noah Leatherland

©2024
BookLife Publishing Ltd.
King's Lynn, Norfolk
PE30 4LS, UK

All rights reserved.
Printed in India.

A catalogue record for this
book is available
from the British Library.

ISBN 978-1-80505-683-6

Written by
Noah Leatherland

Edited by
Robin Twiddy

Designed by
Drue Rintoul

All facts, statistics, web addresses and URLs in this book were verified as valid and accurate at time of writing.
No responsibility for any changes to external websites or references can be accepted by either the author or publisher.

AN INTRODUCTION TO BOOKLIFE RAPID READERS...

Packed full of gripping topics and twisted tales, BookLife Rapid Readers are perfect for older children looking to propel their reading up to top speed. With three levels based on our planet's fastest animals, children will be able to find the perfect point from which to accelerate their reading journey. From the spooky to the silly, these roaring reads will turn every child at every reading level into a prolific page-turner!

CHEETAH
The fastest animals on land, cheetahs will be taking their first strides as they race to top speed.

MARLIN
The fastest animals under water, marlins will be blasting through their journey.

FALCON
The fastest animals in the air, falcons will be flying at top speed as they tear through the skies.

IMAGE CREDITS

All images courtesy of Shutterstock.com. With thanks to Getty Images, Thinkstock Photo and iStockphoto. Cover – tsuneomp, Sergio Photone, Here, Jakub Krechowicz, sociologas, wabeno. Recurring – Elizaveta Mironets, sociologas, wabeno. P1 – tsuneomp. P4–5 – Pavlo Baliukh, Romolo Tavani. P6–7 – Pressmaster, Tithi Luadthong P8–9 – Kim Wilson, FOTOKITA. P10–11 – Dragana Gordic, CREATISTA. P12–13 – FOTOKITA, Paradise studio. P14–15 – Edit 4 Me, FOTOKITA. P16–17 – Maris Grunskis, N. Steele. P18–19 – Kiselev Andrey Valerevich, Morphius Film. P20–21 – Nebojsa Markovic, Deborah Kolb. P22–23 – Tithi Luadthong, Kiselev Andrey Valerevich. P24–25 – Stepan Kapl, FOTOKITA. P26–27 – Teno3, leolintang. P28–29 – leolintang, Kiselev Andrey Valerevich. P30 – Fer Gregory.

CONTENTS

PAGE 4	What Is a Life Cycle?
PAGE 6	What Is a Zombie?
PAGE 8	The Curse Begins
PAGE 10	The Early Zombie
PAGE 12	The Fully Transformed Zombie
PAGE 14	Diet
PAGE 16	Habitat
PAGE 18	The Old Zombie
PAGE 20	Passing on the Curse
PAGE 22	Types of Zombie
PAGE 24	Spotting a Zombie
PAGE 26	How to Deal with a Zombie
PAGE 28	Life Cycle of a Zombie
PAGE 30	Beware the Paranormal!
PAGE 31	Glossary
PAGE 32	Index

Words that look like <u>this</u> can be found in the glossary on page **31**.

WHAT IS A LIFE CYCLE?

Every living thing has a life cycle. During their life cycle, a living thing changes and grows. There are different stages to each living thing's life cycle.

Living things <u>reproduce</u> to keep the life cycle going. It is normal for living things to die as part of their life cycle.

However, some things in this world are not normal. They are nothing like anything else on the planet. They are paranormal.

Some paranormal beings start as normal living things. Death is only the beginning for these creatures. They live and die... and live again!

This is exactly how the gory life cycle of the zombie begins.

WHAT IS A ZOMBIE?

Zombies have terrified people for a long time. Stories about dead creatures coming back to life have been told for thousands of years.

Nobody is sure where the first zombie came from. Some people think that evil magic was used to bring the first zombie back from the dead. Since then, the curse has spread all over the world.

Zombies are definitely not alive, but they are more than just dead. They are <u>undead</u>. Their hearts do not beat, but their brains work just enough for their bodies to shuffle around.

Zombies have a life cycle just like every other creature. Learning about their life cycle could be the key to staying out of their reach.

THE CURSE BEGINS

Anybody can be cursed to become a zombie. Getting cursed by a zombie is a painful and bloody ordeal. It only takes one bite for the horror to begin.

It is a moment of fright. The tight grip of hungry hands. A feeling of dread. The stench of rot… and then jagged teeth sinking into <u>flesh</u>!

A person is lucky to get away from a zombie with just one bite taken out of them. But that one bite will change this person's life… and end it!

If they are quick, chopping off the body part that has been bitten might stop the curse. If not, they will start to change…

THE EARLY ZOMBIE

A person bitten by a zombie does not <u>transform</u> into an undead monster straight away. It could take a few hours or just a few minutes.

First, they will start to feel dizzy and will not be able to tell which way is up. They will start to cough and feel sick as the curse takes over their body.

The cursed person will soon become very unwell. They will feel very faint and eventually they will die... but not for long.

They will start to move again. They will no longer be sick or dizzy. Instead, they will start to shuffle around, looking to take a bite out of something... or someone!

The Fully Transformed Zombie

Now that they have risen from the dead, the cursed person has become a zombie. They are still able to move and shamble around.

There is only one thing that zombies think about – the taste of warm flesh. It is the only thing they are interested in, and they will do anything they can to get it.

Zombies might look weak, but do not be fooled. They are shockingly strong. A zombie will stop at nothing to get a bite of living human flesh.

If a zombie gets hold of someone, it is usually over. It is hard to pull yourself free from their grip. Do not let them get a hold of you!

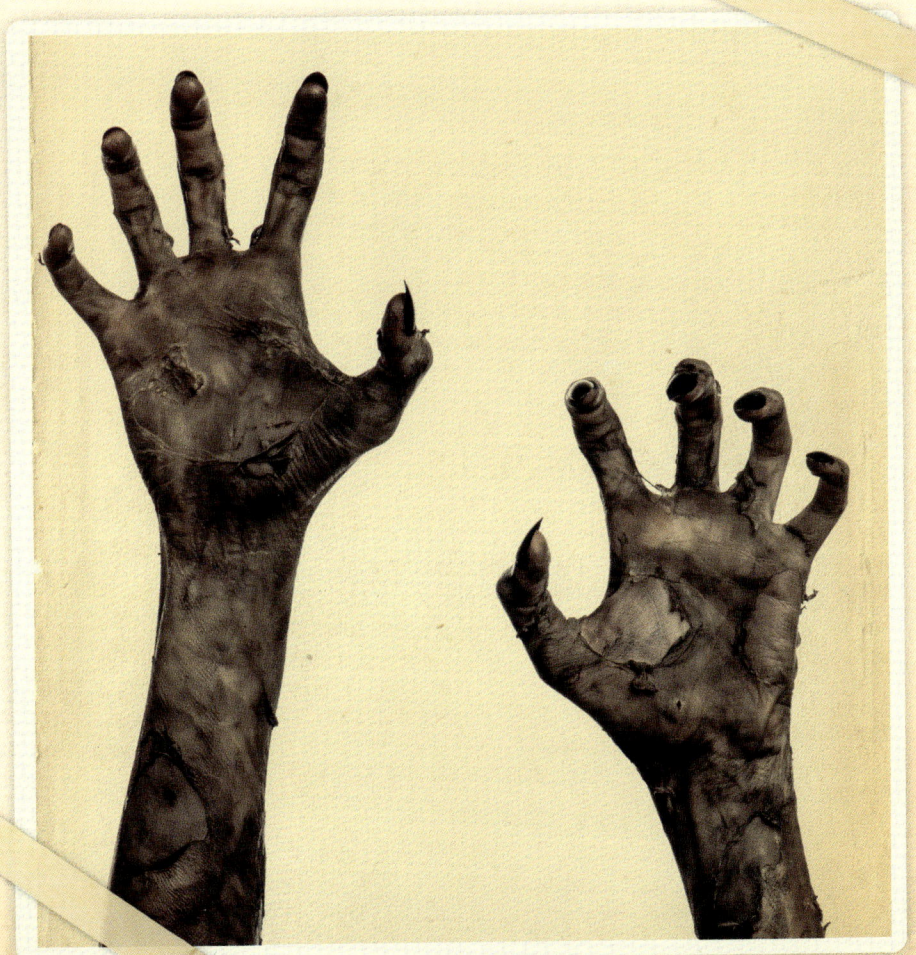

DIET

There is only one thing that makes up the zombie's diet – you.

Zombies eat every part of a person they can. They will chomp on the skin, the muscles and the <u>organs</u>, but their favourite part is the brain.

Some people think zombies eat brains because they have a lot of <u>nutrients</u> that keep their dead bodies strong.

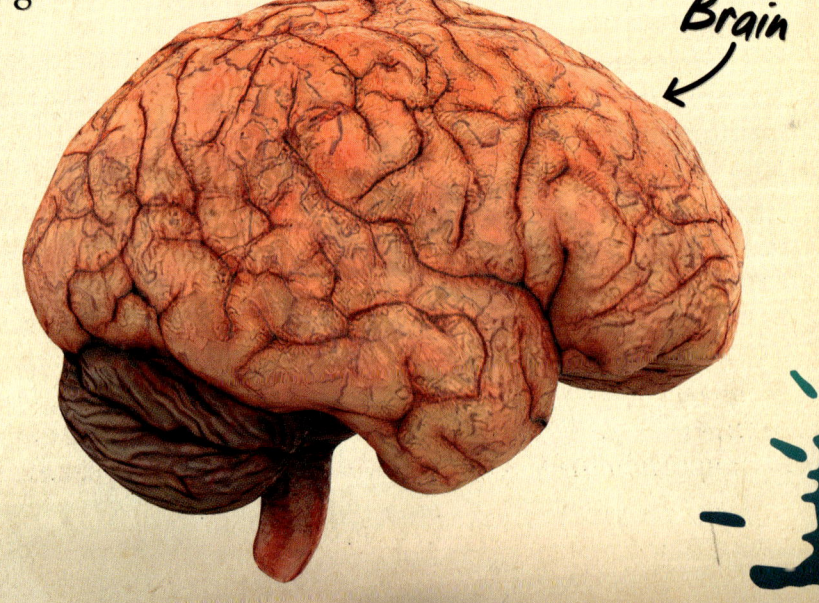

Brain

Zombies do not just eat people. If they can catch them, zombies will eat the flesh of animals too.

When living things eat food, their organs <u>digest</u> it. A zombie's organs do not work because its body is dead. So, the flesh it eats just sits inside its stomach where it slowly rots away.

HABITAT

Zombies have been found in all sorts of places. They have been spotted in cities, out in the countryside, near the beach and all over the world.

Some people believe that zombies go to places that they liked when they were alive. For example, if the person liked to go shopping, they might hang around shopping malls as a zombie.

Zombies do not tend to stay in one place for long. Zombies are drawn to places where they can find food. So, zombies are usually found in places near lots of humans.

When zombies go looking for food, they join up with other zombies. A large group of zombies is called a herd.

THE OLD ZOMBIE

Zombies do not grow as they get older. Instead, they break down because their bodies are already dead. Lots of things can happen to a zombie as they start to fall apart.

Zombies start to rot from the inside out. <u>Bacteria</u> eats away at what is left of the zombie's skin, flesh and organs, making them look like a gory mess.

A person's skeleton is held together by the fleshy parts around it. So, as the zombie's body starts to rot, their skeleton comes apart too. Lots of zombies' arms and legs end up falling off.

Some zombies barely have any body left after a few years. They might look just like skeletons towards the end of their life cycle.

Passing on
The Curse

When zombies catch sight of something they can bite a chunk out of, they do not stop. One zombie hunting for food can soon be joined by more and more zombies.

Zombies are most dangerous when they are moving in herds. Herds of zombies can surround buildings and break through barriers. That is a lot of hungry mouths.

As well as being hungry for flesh, zombies want to pass on the curse. They need to make more zombies to carry on the life cycle.

A zombie's bite does not need to be very deep in order to pass on the curse. As long as their rotten teeth can break through the skin, then the curse is passed on.

Types of Zombie

Some different kinds of zombies might be shambling in a herd.

Fast Zombies

Some zombies can move much faster than others. This might be because they were very fit and active when they were alive. Or perhaps their hunger for flesh is so strong that it makes them run for food.

Either way, fast zombies are some of the most dangerous.

SMART ZOMBIES

Sometimes, a zombie's brain is a bit more active than others. This might happen because the zombie was very smart when they were alive.

Smart zombies can do things that other zombies have forgotten how to do. They might be able to open doors or climb things. Some of them might even figure out how to use weapons!

SPOTTING A ZOMBIE

Although it might be easy to spot a zombie when they are falling apart, freshly bitten zombies can be harder to tell apart.

EYES

Take a look at their eyes. If their eyes are blank and cloudy, the curse has already taken over.

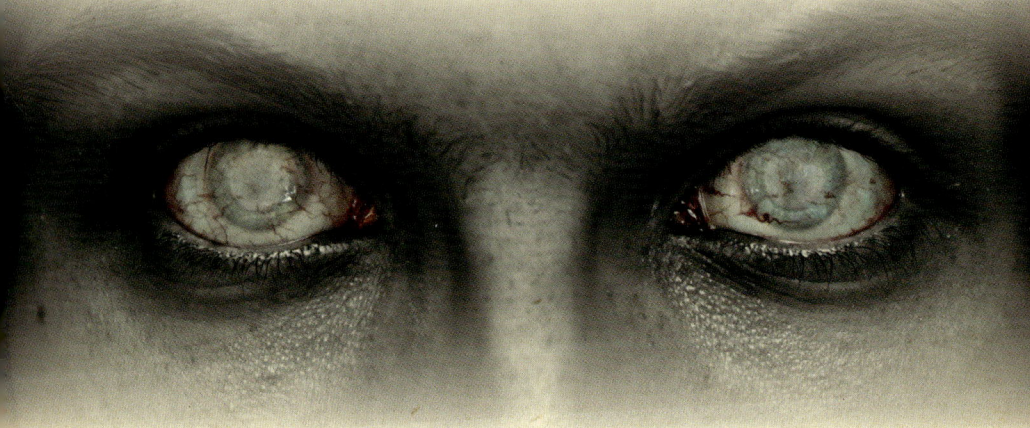

SMELL

The zombie might have started to break down. If someone smells rotten, they might be a zombie.

MOUTH

Zombies are always looking to sink their teeth into some juicy flesh. If someone's mouth is hanging open, they might be getting ready to bite.

GROANS

Zombies groan a lot. Some people think zombies groan because they are so hungry. Others say that if you listen closely, they are actually saying what they are hungry for – "Braaaaaiiiiiiinsssssss."

How to Deal with a Zombie

Coming face to face with a zombie can be frightening. It is important to stay calm so that you can deal with them.

Things that hurt other creatures will not harm a zombie. Zombies do not feel any pain and they do not feel fear. What might work with other creatures will not work with zombies.

Some people may think that fire is a good way of getting rid of herds of zombies. All this will do is make a herd of flaming zombies to run away from.

There is one thing that will definitely get rid of a zombie. All you need to do is destroy a zombie's brain and they will return to the grave.

LIFE CYCLE OF A ZOMBIE

The zombie's life cycle starts with a bite that passes on the curse. Someone who has been bitten might be able to hold off the curse for a little while. However, no one can escape it.

Soon enough, they will die, and the zombie's curse will make them undead. Then, the hunger begins, and they crave human flesh.

As the zombie shambles around, its dead body begins to fall apart. Its skin peels off and its guts fall out in a bloody mess. It might lose an arm, a leg or both!

Before it totally rots away, a zombie might bite an unlucky person. This passes on the curse, and the zombie's life cycle carries on.

BEWARE THE PARANORMAL!

Zombies are not the only creepy creatures out there. There are all kinds of scary paranormal creatures with their own life cycles lurking in the shadows.

As tempting as it might be to go looking for them, be careful! These paranormal creatures can be very dangerous. It is best to read about them and learn how to stay safe!

GLOSSARY

BACTERIA   tiny living things, too small to see, that can cause diseases

CRAVE   to really want something

DIGEST   to break down food into things that can be absorbed and used by the body

FLESH   the soft tissue of a body

NUTRIENTS   natural substances that plants and animals need to grow and stay healthy

ORGANS   parts of a living thing that have a specific, important function

REPRODUCE   to make more of the same thing

PARANORMAL   something that cannot be explained by science

TRANSFORM   to turn into something else

UNDEAD   dead but still able to move around

INDEX

BACTERIA 18

BRAINS 7, 14, 23, 27

GROANS 25

HERDS 17, 20, 22, 27

MUSCLES 14

ORGANS 14–15, 18

SKELETONS 19

SKIN 14, 18, 21, 29

TEETH 8, 21, 25